THE SOUND OF MUSIC

CONTENTS

— PIANO LEVEL —
INTERMEDIATE

ISBN 978-1-4803-4291-0

WILLIAMSON MUSIC®

AN IMAGEM COMPANY™
www.williamsonmusic.com

EXCLUSIVELY DISTRIBUTED BY

HAL•LEONARD®
CORPORATION
7777 W. BLUEMOUND RD. P.O. BOX 13819 MILWAUKEE, WI 53213

In Australia Contact:
Hal Leonard Australia Pty. Ltd.
4 Lentara Court
Cheltenham, Victoria, 3192 Australia
Email: ausadmin@halleonard.com.au

Visit Hal Leonard Online at
www.halleonard.com

Visit Phillip at
www.phillipkeveren.com

CLIMB EV'RY MOUNTAIN

Lyrics by OSCAR HAMMERSTEIN II
Music by RICHARD RODGERS
Arranged by Phillip Keveren

Like a prayer (♩ = 96)

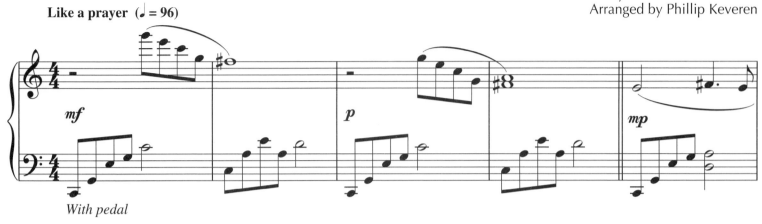

With pedal

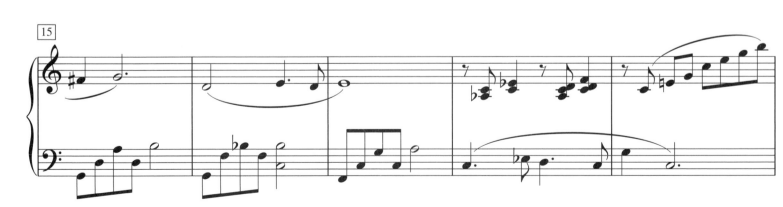

EDELWEISS

Lyrics by OSCAR HAMMERSTEIN II
Music by RICHARD RODGERS
Arranged by Phillip Keveren

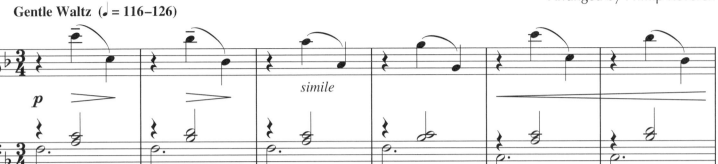

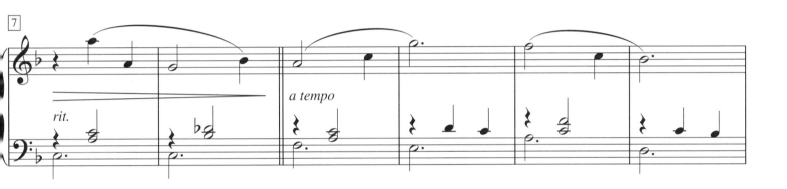

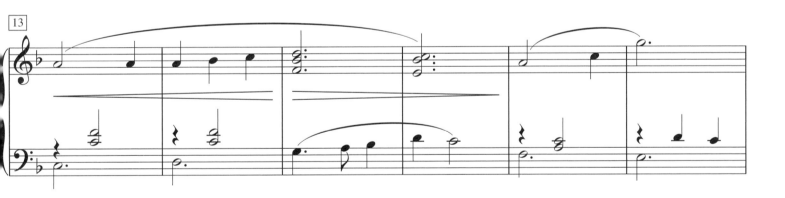

DO-RE-MI

Lyrics by OSCAR HAMMERSTEIN II
Music by RICHARD RODGERS
Arranged by Phillip Keveren

I HAVE CONFIDENCE

Lyrics and Music by
RICHARD RODGERS
Arranged by Phillip Keveren

THE LONELY GOATHERD

Lyrics by OSCAR HAMMERSTEIN II
Music by RICHARD RODGERS
Arranged by Phillip Keveren

MARIA

Lyrics by OSCAR HAMMERSTEIN II
Music by RICHARD RODGERS
Arranged by Phillip Keveren

Briskly, in 1 (♩. = 100)

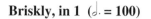

23

AN ORDINARY COUPLE

<blockquote>

Lyrics by OSCAR HAMMERSTEIN II
Music by RICHARD RODGERS
Arranged by Phillip Keveren
</blockquote>

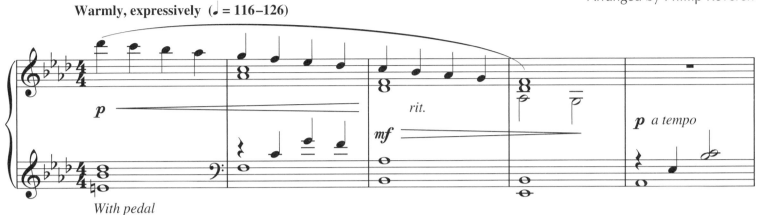

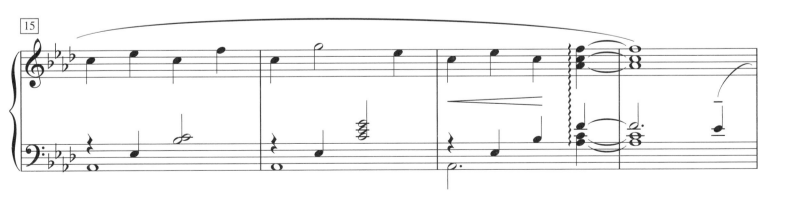

MY FAVORITE THINGS

Lyrics by OSCAR HAMMERSTEIN II
Music by RICHARD RODGERS
Arranged by Phillip Keveren

Sprightly, with motion

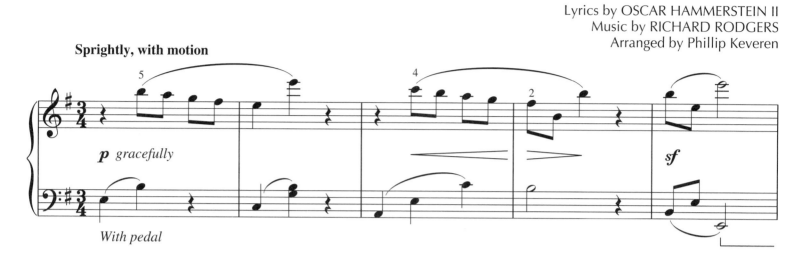

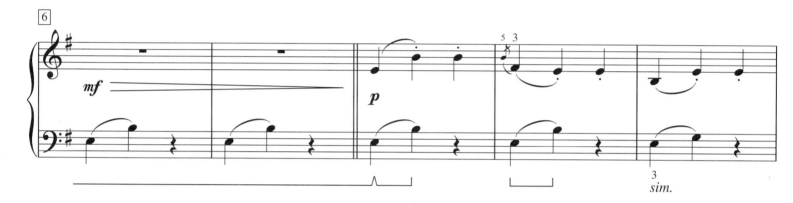

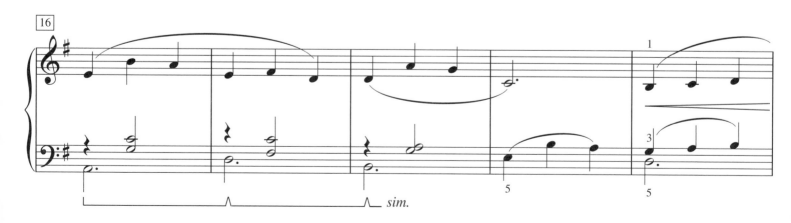

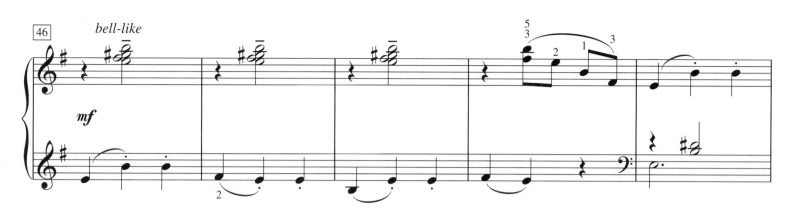

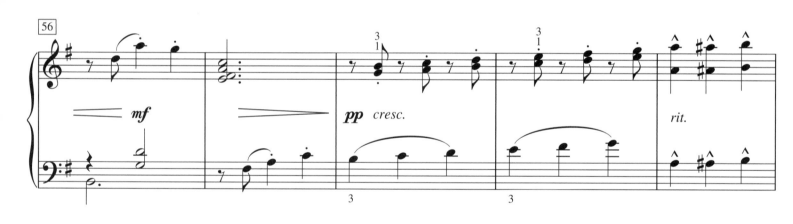

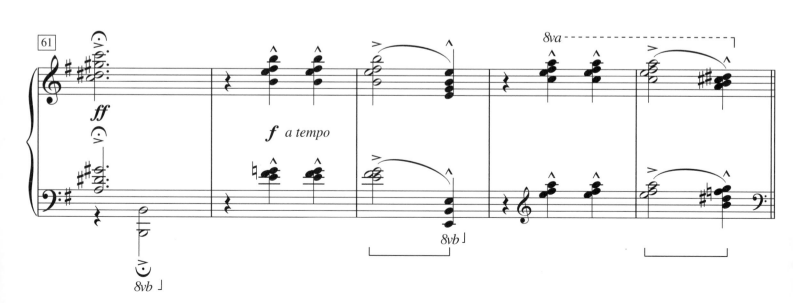

SIXTEEN GOING ON SEVENTEEN

Lyrics by OSCAR HAMMERSTEIN II
Music by RICHARD RODGERS
Arranged by Phillip Keveren

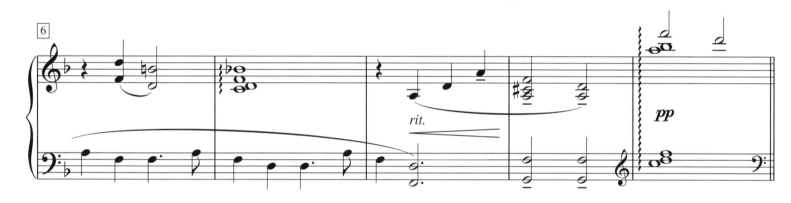

SOMETHING GOOD

Lyrics and Music by
RICHARD RODGERS
Arranged by Phillip Keveren

SO LONG, FAREWELL

Lyrics by OSCAR HAMMERSTEIN II
Music by RICHARD RODGERS
Arranged by Phillip Keveren

Bell-like (♩ = 116)

WEDDING PROCESSIONAL

Lyrics by OSCAR HAMMERSTEIN II
Music by RICHARD RODGERS
Arranged by Phillip Keveren

THE SOUND OF MUSIC

Lyrics by OSCAR HAMMERSTEIN II
Music by RICHARD RODGERS
Arranged by Phillip Keveren

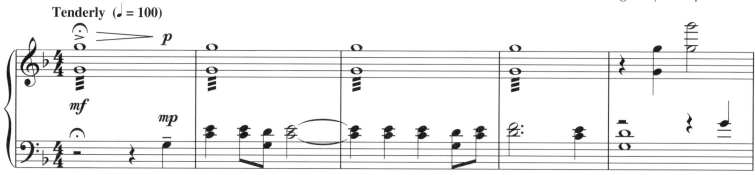